Reignite Your Spirit!

A Companion Guide to
Anticipate God's Goodness:
Letters of Encouragement
to Ignite Your Spirit

Gaye Lindfors

Printed in the United States of America

Cover & Interior Design Elements by String Marketing, Inc. | Interior Formatting by Dallas Hodge | Publishing Support by Cher Stein, The Write Perspective

Hi Friend!
I'm so glad you're here!

Imagine waking up each morning, saying Yes! to God, and walking through your day *anticipating* His goodness. No more waiting, wondering, or wishing for things to be different. Just a heart that's ready to move forward, trusting that God is already at work.

It's easy to lose our sense of anticipation, isn't it? Life gets busy. Or boring. Or just *too much*. So we start putting off truly *living*. Telling ourselves we'll engage later, when things settle down. But here's the truth. **Life happens in the everyday moments.** Wouldn't it be more fulfilling (and fun!) to fully *engage* in life—living, doing, and experiencing—rather than just observing and whispering *What if I ...?*

So here's my invitation. **Say Yes to God. Anticipate His goodness. Then get up, go, and keep going!** Let's **embrace the promises** God has made, **focus on the people** He's placed in our path, and **step into the work** He's showing us each day.

Maybe some of what you read in *Anticipate God's Goodness: Letters of Encouragement to Ignite Your Spirit* wasn't brand-new. I hope this companion guide **reminds you of those truths in fresh ways**, and **encourages you to actually *live* what you know!**

Anticipate God's Goodness was such a fun book to write. It came straight from my heart! And now, I'm excited to share this companion guide with you.

Let's Reignite Your Spirit!

Dear Lord, bless the woman who is reading this guide. May she be strengthened by the promises from your Word and choose to continue to say yes to you. Give her courage to turn away from anything that keeps her from living the full life you've promised her. Give her the desire to know you better.

Teach her, O God, how to anticipate your goodness. Reignite her spirit as she walks with you.

Open her ears to hear your call and open her heart to respond with ...

I am saying yes to God.
I will get up. I will go.
I will keep going.

A Guide to Your Guide

How to Use Your
Reignite Your Spirit! Companion Guide

This guide is designed to help you engage more deeply with *Anticipate God's Goodness: Letters of Encouragement to Ignite Your Spirit*. I pray that as you go through these pages, something shifts in your heart and mind—that you feel refreshed, reenergized, and ready to keep going.

Stop waiting for life to show up.
Show up and discover the good life God has for you.
Anticipate his goodness!

One Guide, Two Ways to Soak It In

I created this guide with you in mind, whether you're someone who loves to reflect on *Anticipate God's Goodness* **letter by letter**, or you are interested in considering the **threads of encouragement** that run through the letters and the themes that tie them together. Both formats are designed to meet you right where you are.

Letter-by-Letter Encouragement (28 sessions)

Walk through *Anticipate God's Goodness* one letter at a time in 28 thoughtful sessions. This format invites you to pause, linger, and let the encouragement in each letter settle deep into your soul.

Perfect for **personal study or one-on-one conversations**, this slower-paced journey gives you the freedom to reflect at your own rhythm, in your favorite chair, on your lunch break, or whenever you need a quiet moment with God. It's an intimate, Spirit-led path, ideal for the seasons when you need to be refreshed, restored, and reignited from the inside out.

Themes of Encouragement (5 sessions)

This format weaves the letters into five meaningful sessions built around three core themes. You'll still read every letter and enjoy the personal stories, steady hope, and heartfelt encouragement tucked into each note. But you'll also follow the key themes that rise to the surface. Truths that will remind you of **God's goodness and faithfulness.**

This format is a purposeful, connected way to experience *Anticipate God's Goodness*. Perfect for **Bible studies, book clubs, virtual group conversations, or any season when meaningful connection with other women** is just what your spirit needs to reignite.

Whether you like to pause on every letter or gather the key messages, this guide gives you both. You're invited to draw near, dig deep, and discover something new! **Choose the rhythm that meets you in your season.**

Suggestions for Moving Through the Companion Guide

- **Keep your Bible open.** Look up the Scriptures and jot down notes.

  > I use several translations and commentaries when I study. And yes, I Google questions and use my phone's dictionary! Whatever helps me dig deeper into the Word.

- **Ask God to open your heart.** Every morning before I study, I pray Acts 16:14: *"Lord, open my heart to pay attention to what you're doing and teaching me."*

- **Keep a journal.** Write down your thoughts, prayers, and the ways your heart and mind are shifting.

Oh, friend, I pray this *Reignite Your Spirit! Companion Guide* **encourages your heart** as you **grow in your faith** and **deepen your relationship with God.** I'd love to hear about your discoveries, reminders, and lessons along the way!

With love and gratitude,

Gaye

Letter-by-Letter Encouragement

A Letter from Gaye

"So here's what I want you to do, God helping you: Take your everyday, ordinary life—your sleeping, eating, going-to-work, and walking-around life—and place it before God as an offering. Embracing what God does for you is the best thing you can do for him."

Romans 12:1-2 (MSG)

Isn't it funny how God sometimes uses the most unexpected moments to show us exactly what we need? Like that day at the triathlon, watching those brave, incredibly cool women show up in their mall swimsuits and regular bikes. What hit me in that moment wasn't their fancy gear (because there wasn't any). It was their courage to do something without waiting for perfect conditions. They weren't standing on the sidelines until they had professional equipment or elite bodies. They just went for it! And I realized. That's exactly what I needed to see.

God's got good things planned for you right now, in your gloriously imperfect state. What if you stopped waiting for a great life to magically appear and instead showed up and said, *Let's go!*?

Don't miss the adventure of walking with God while anticipating his goodness! (Swimsuits not required.)

Dear Friend, Your Thoughts?

- Like the women racing in the triathlon, stepping out of your comfort zone isn't easy. Have you done something brave, even if you weren't ready? How did it feel?

- Think back to a time when you felt weary or stuck. What helped you get unstuck?

- What "race" in your life feels daunting right now? What fears or excuses are holding you back from taking action? What Bible verses—truths—can replace those fears?

Don't wait for life
to show up.
Show up and
discover the life
God has for you!

Day by Day

"Don't be afraid, for I am with you. Don't be discouraged,
for I am your God. I will strengthen you and help you. I will
hold you up with my victorious right hand."

Isaiah 41:10 (NLT)

Life's a lot like running. Sometimes it's a graceful stride, and sometimes it's a wheezing shuffle to the finish line. Don't we know it! But here's the thing. God is in every single step, giving strength for today, and maybe even a second wind for tomorrow.

I hope this letter encouraged you to lean into God's grace and trust him for your next step. Whether you're lacing up for a 5K or just trying to make it through the day without collapsing, this one's for you.

Keep going, friend.

Dear Friend, Your Thoughts?

- Where do you need God to strengthen you today? Where do you need his help?

- The song "Day by Day" is a reminder of God's presence. Is there a verse, hymn, or phrase that helps you stay grounded in your faith? How can you use it in your everyday life? (Another one of my favorite "keep going" songs: "Press On" by Selah. WOW!)

- On page 20 in *Anticipate God's Goodness*, you'll find the first verse to "Day by Day." Rewrite that verse in your own words. Make it personal.

In the little annoyances and the big trials, God whispers: "Let's do this together."

Plow the Field

*"Plow up the hard ground of your hearts!
Do not waste your good seed among thorns."*

Jeremiah 4:3 (NLT)

Oh my word, can we talk about those times when life needs a good plowing? You know what I mean. Those seasons when everything feels a bit weedy and overgrown, and your heart could use some serious turning over? (Trust me, I've been there!) It's like my sister's adventure on the John Deere tractor as she sings "Puppy Love."

Sometimes we get so caught up in our own little world that our rows get a bit crooked. And over time we stop paying attention to the thistle and crabgrass that are putting down roots.

But here's the thing. God's got some fresh, life-giving seeds to plant, and we're going to make room for them. Just imagine all the new life that will spring up!

Let's plow!

Dear Friend, Your Thoughts?

- At the end of this letter, I offered two voices to help you get plowing (the kind lady who sits next to you in church, or the pastor in the red suspenders). Which Encouraging Voice are you most likely to respond to? Why?

- What "weeds" in your life are draining your energy or taking your attention away from your relationship with God? They could be hurts, messes, sins, someone else's actions, etc. What do you need to do to get rid of those weeds? (Seek forgiveness? Apologize? Confess and repent? Forgive? Make a change?)

- Think about a time when you did the hard work of clearing out unhealthy patterns, influences, or sins in your life. You plowed your field. What new growth came as a result?

*Plow the field.
Don't let the weeds
set up a new zip
code in your heart.*

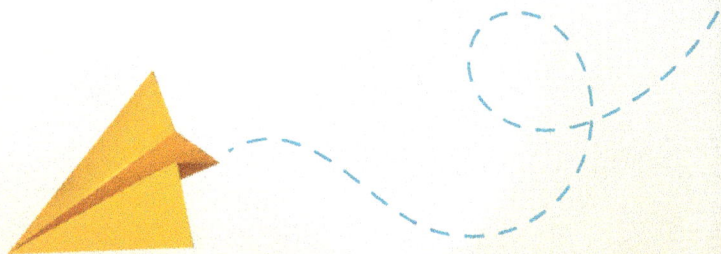

Fill 'er Up!

*"You have bedded me down in lush meadows, you find me quiet
pools to drink from. True to your word, you let me catch my
breath and send me in the right direction."*

Psalm 23:2-3 (MSG)

Feeling drained and running on empty? You're not alone. Sometimes life feels like one long stretch of road with the gas light blinking, doesn't it? Here's your friendly reminder to pull over and refuel. Reach out to your Orville—the person who shows up for you with help and encouragement. Check into your pit stop, and give yourself the space to pause, breathe, and rest.

The irony is, when I look closer at my own empty tank moments, I've often discovered something surprising. More often than we'd like to admit, our energy is low because we've filled our tanks with activities and time wasters that don't actually nourish us. Consider what's best to fill up your tank!

And remember: Don't ever underestimate the power of a good nap.

Dear Friend, Your Thoughts?

- What are the warning signs that your "tank" is running low? How do you typically respond when you're feeling drained? What do you do to refill that tank? Does it work?

- What activities, people, or practices bring you the most energy and joy? How can you make more time for them in your daily life?

- Psalm 23 is so refreshing, isn't it? What do "quiet pools" and "lush meadows" look like for you? Where do you find them?

Stop running on empty.
Ask God to refuel your
spirit. Take a nap.

Pop the Bubbles

"Thank God because He's good,
because his love never quits."

Psalm 118:1 (MSG)

Have you ever noticed how those pesky feelings of guilt and shame can bubble up out of nowhere? Like that sweet little girl in church with her yellow daisy barrette. One sharp word and suddenly the sunshine dims. We've all been there, haven't we? Those moments when we feel small and want to shrink into ourselves?

But here's what's amazing. When you've messed up or disappointed someone, God isn't standing there with a finger-snapping, shushing attitude. Nope! He's the one with open arms saying, *Come here. I love you.* Then he wraps his arms around you, offering you grace and mercy to start again.

You are loved and cared for by a faithful, compassionate God. His love never quits.

Dear Friend, Your Thoughts?

- Think about someone whose faith seems strong, and she always brings the joy. If you peeked into her soul, what do you think you'd see?

- When feelings of shame or humiliation hit, what's your go-to response? And when those moments come (because we all face them), what steps could you take to respond in a healthier way? How might you replace those negative thoughts and lies with the truth of who God says you are?

- Who in your life needs a reminder that God is an open-arms, embracing God? How can you share that message with her this week?

God isn't a finger-pointing, shushing God. He's an open-arms, embracing God.

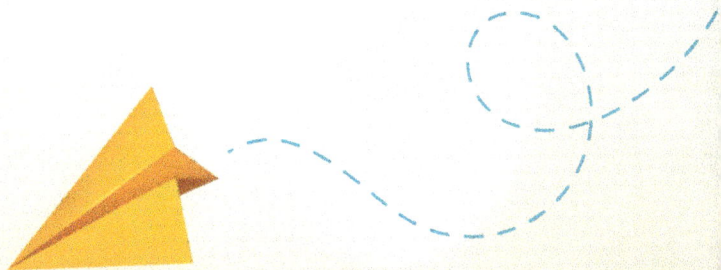

The Sync Swimmers

"Two are better than one because a good return comes when two work together. If one of them falls, the other can help him up."

Ecclesiastes 4:9-10 (VOICE)

Okay. About my synchronized swimming adventure. Good grief. Who attempts that without practicing in actual water? But you know, our fabulous, frolicsome fiasco was a beautiful reminder. We need friends who will give us a nudge when we're stuck, a boost when we're weary, and wipe away the fog in our goggles when we need to see life a little more clearly.

I'm pretty sure that you know how to nudge, boost, and bring the encouragement when your friend needs it. It's harder to ask for the boost, right?

Friend, ask for the help.

Dear Friend, Your Thoughts?

- When did someone "sync swim" with you? How did her support impact your life?

- What holds you back from reaching out when you're having a hard time? How might you reframe your thinking to see that asking for help isn't a weakness, but actually a strength?

- Think about someone in your life who might need a little push or a gentle lift this week. How can you reach out and offer support?

Sometimes we
need a gentle lift;
other times, we give it.
Either way,
we're better together.

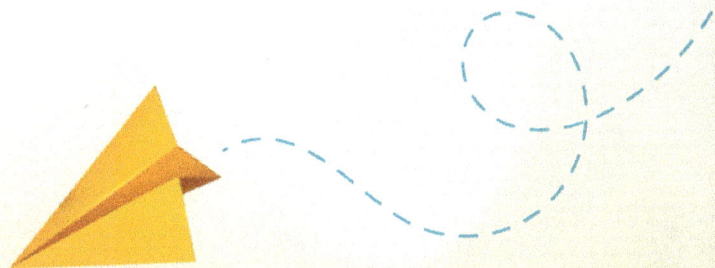

You Belong Here

"Do not be afraid or discouraged, for the Lord will personally go ahead of you. He will be with you; he will neither fail you nor abandon you."

Deuteronomy 31:8 (NLT)

Have you ever seen a turkey strut with confidence? Recently, a gaggle of them stopped right in front of our car and initiated a stare down against our bumper. Talk about confidence overload!

We never want to enter a room leading with our egos. But remember, you absolutely belong in the places God has called you. No second-guessing needed! You can walk forward with complete confidence in his direction and strength, knowing you are representing him.

Take another look at the Israelites' missed opportunity in Numbers 13. It sure makes me want to embrace a fresh perspective on stepping forward with faith.

Leave fear behind and walk boldly into the spaces God has prepared for you. He has wonderful things planned just for you!

Dear Friend, Your Thoughts?

- We've all had those moments when we wonder if we belong in a particular room or situation. When have you felt that way? What's behind that feeling?

- What truth can you whisper to yourself when you feel like you don't belong? Here's a suggestion: *God has placed me here, so I belong here. I'm going to make a difference.* What other "I belong here" affirmations would you add?

- How can you bring light and encouragement to others who may not be feeling comfortable in the spaces you are in? (You've got something to offer them!)

We are not grasshoppers
with a grasshopper god.
We are daughters of
the King of Kings!
When God leads us somewhere
let's step right into it.
No one else is allowed to tell us
if we're good enough
to enter that room.

Listen for The Truth

"I am leaving you with a gift—peace of mind and heart."

John 14:27 (NLT)

You know those jack-in-the-box toys that make you jump even when you know what's coming? Discouragement can be just like that, right? There you are, bouncing along nicely, then POP! Suddenly Jack's bobbing its scary red head at you, whispering all those unwelcome thoughts. Been there? Me too.

But here's the thing that makes me smile. While we're busy listening to that squeaky toy voice, God's over here saying, *Hey beloved, I've got something better to tell you!*

How about shoving Discouraging Jack back in its box. Listen to The One who lives to fill you with hope and love.

Dear Friend, Your Thoughts?

- Make a note about a time when God's promises gave you hope in the middle of discouragement. The God who was faithful then, is the same God who is faithful today!

- Discouragement can feel subtle and sneaky. How can you remain alert to recognize it? How will you shove it back into its box when you recognize it?

- John 14:27 speaks about the gift of peace Jesus gives us. What steps can you take to claim that peace in your daily life?

Let God wrap His arms around you.
Hear Him say, "I've got you. We're doing life together. Hope in Me. Trust Me."

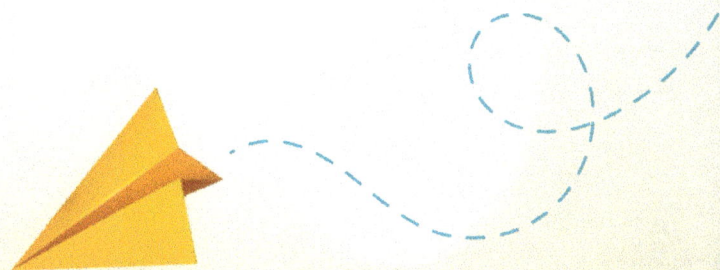

Getting Settled

"The Lord is my shepherd; I have all that I need ...
for you are close beside me."

Psalm 23:1,4 (NLT)

Can we talk about those nights when our brains refuse to shut off? When it's like having 47 browser tabs open while a dozen radio stations play at once. None of them tuned in clearly, but all demanding attention. Ooftah. In those moments, we need to stop the circling and swirling of our thoughts.

Remember. God always gives you what you need. He can handle your mental chaos and the noise. He settles your mind, calms your heart, and removes your anxiety. Invite him into your restless thoughts.

Pause. Take a breath. And then, turn your attention to the Prince of Peace, asking him to close all the tabs while you settle into his presence and focus on his promises. He is so faithful. Calming. Settling.

Dear Friend, Your Thoughts?

- What happens when you try to control others and fix situations using only your limited wisdom and strength? How has it impacted your relationships? What healthier alternative would allow you to help while strengthening connections rather than straining them?

- When you feel unsettled or anxious, what practical steps can you take to invite God into those moments?

- What Bible verses help you settle your heart when life feels chaotic? Take a few minutes to find them and write them down.

Settle your unsettled.
Let go of the swirling.
Invite God into this moment.
Your life will change.

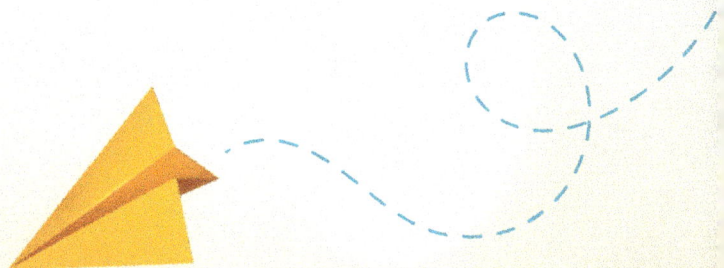

Happy Birthday

*"You direct me on the path that leads to a beautiful life.
As I walk with You, the pleasures are never-ending,
and I know true joy and contentment."*

Psalm 16:11 (VOICE)

Birthdays aren't just about getting older. They're about celebrating the gift of life God has given us. How fabulous is that perspective? So what if we've got a few more laugh lines than we used to. They're proof that we've been living this life with gusto!

Celebrate the gift in every season of your life on this side of heaven. (Cake is optional, but I highly recommend it. With ice cream, obviously.)

I'm so glad you were born!

Dear Friend, Your Thoughts?

- How do you typically feel about celebrating your birthday? Why?

  ➤ If birthdays aren't your happy place, how might you shift your focus to celebrating God's gift of life?

- Think about the unique ways you bring joy to others. How can you continue to share those gifts this year?

- John 10:10 speaks of a full and abundant life. What does that look like for you? How can you experience it in your everyday?

My laugh lines and
wrinkles prove it:
I have truly lived!

When the Ducks Don't Cooperate

"So be careful how you live; be mindful of your steps."

Ephesians 5:15 (VOICE)

Life rarely goes as planned, and sometimes the ducks refuse to get in a row. But neither perfection nor control are the goals, right? Trusting God in the middle of the chaos? That's where the good stuff happens. But isn't it interesting how we keep trying to fix what we were never meant to fix.

Here's something worth holding on to. God has assigned us the work he wants us to do. We are responsible for our work, not for everyone else's work. And let's not forget, God is God. We are not. (That's a good one, isn't it?)

We won't go wrong when we keep our God-connection secure, walking in his presence!

Dear Friend, Your Thoughts?

- What areas of your life feel like you're trying to get your ducks in a row? How can you release control and trust God's guidance?

- Dallas Willard encourages us to arrange our days to "experience total contentment, joy, and confidence ... with God."* How can you incorporate this perspective into your daily life?

- Psalm 116:9 reminds us to walk in the Lord's presence. What practices help you stay connected to him throughout your day?

---

* John Ortberg, *Soul Keeping: Caring for the Most Important Part of You* (Grand Rapids, Michigan: Zondervan, 2014), 98.

I don't have all, not even some, of my ducks in a row. But they are all in the same pond, so I have that going for me ... which is cool.

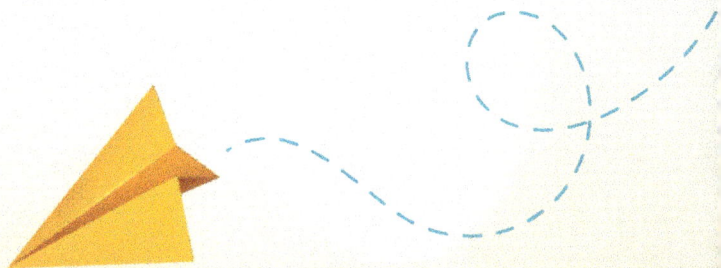

Stop Struggling

*"He reached down from on high and took hold of me;
he pulled me out of deep water."*

Psalm 18:16 (CSB)

Do you ever talk back to the perky instructor in the online workout video? (Please tell me I'm not the only one.) When I was fighting with my "bat wings," trying to figure out which leg was my left one while arguing with the instructor, it hit me. I was treating life's storms the same way. You know what I mean?

Instead of floating with God's grace and trusting his faithfulness through the tough stuff, I was out there shaking a fist at God, and throwing punches at the waves like that would somehow make them behave. Why do we fight so hard against things we can't control or fix? *Sigh.*

Let's take a breath, a break, and stop struggling, OK? Leaning into God's strength in our storms is a much better option.

Dear Friend, Your Thoughts?

- What stormy situation are you trying to control right now? That one that is not yours to control. What does God want you to know about this?

- What life jackets can you slip on to keep yourself from sinking?

- When we memorize Bible verses, they become a lifeline we can grasp exactly when we need them. Start by writing this one down, then take time to commit it to memory: *"When you go through deep waters, I will be with you. When you go through rivers of difficulty, you will not drown."* Isaiah 43:2 (NLT)

In every struggle, God reaches through the waves to pull us out into a calmer space. Rest in his strong and faithful arms.

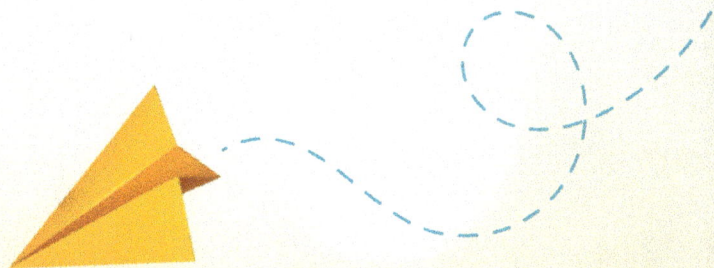

Fairy Tales Can Be Messy

"You [God] have surrounded me on every side, behind me and before me, and You have placed Your hand gently on my shoulder."

Psalm 139:5 (VOICE)

So about those fairy tale expectations we've all experienced at some point in our lives. You know, the ones that promised us perfect hair, eighteen-inch waists, and butterflies perching on our shoulders? It may all sound amazing, but here's the real deal: even Cinderella probably had days when the glass slipper gave her blisters. Life rarely matches our picture-perfect dreams.

When you find yourself whispering into your pillow, *I didn't think my life would be like this*, it might be helpful to look up and see the good things God has placed in front of you. Even when life just makes you shake your head—*I can't believe this is happening*—look for the sliver of goodness. It's out there. Watch for it.

Remember. This season you're in isn't the whole story, it's just a chapter. God knows EXACTLY where you are and where you are going. He's walking with you.

Dear Friend, Your Thoughts?

- What expectations about your life have left you feeling discouraged? How can you shift your focus to see God's goodness in this chapter?

- Here are a few questions and jumpstart ideas to help you get back in sync with the life God has for you. Think about them and make some notes:

  - What's good in my life right now? (*I have a place to live. Friends. Clothes. Memories of good times.*)

  - Who do I want to be? (*Stress free. Energetic. Helpful. Rested. Faithful.*)

  - What will it take for me to become that person? Take your "Who do I want to be" list that you just wrote, and under each attribute, write what you can do to make it happen. (*Focus on the good things. Stop the mindless scrolling. Go to bed earlier. Eat less sugar. Say 'I'm sorry.'*)

God never calls you
to a place where
He is not present.
God never calls you to
a place to be miserable.

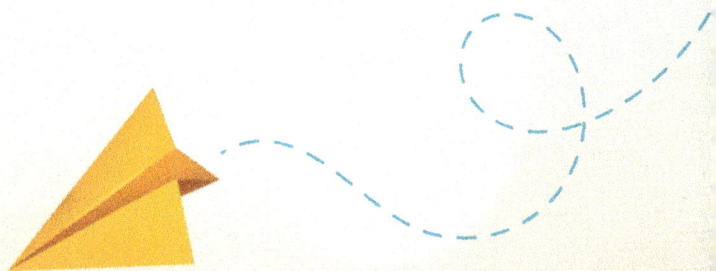

Keep Skipping

"Go out into the world uncorrupted, a breath of fresh air in this squalid and polluted society. Provide people with a glimpse of good living and of the living God."

Philippians 2:15 (MSG)

"Shine like stars in the world."

(CSB)

Have you ever had your joy crushed by someone's careless words? Yep, me too. Just like those kids in the bookstore, skipping with pure joy until someone clapped their hands and stole their sunshine. (Still makes my heart hurt.) It makes me think about all the times I've been a joy-stealer without even realizing it. Quick to criticize or correct.

Joy is fragile, but it's also contagious. I want to be someone who protects it, nurtures it, and passes it on. You too?

Let's bring the breath of fresh air—shine like the stars—reflecting God's joy and grace. Life's going to be sweeter when there's more skipping and less shushing, right?

Dear Friend, Your Thoughts?

- What habits or attitudes can you cultivate to ensure you're bringing joy rather than unintentionally taking it away?

- Madeleine L'Engle writes about showing others a "lovely light." What does that look like in your daily interactions?

- How can you extend grace and kindness to someone who doesn't share your beliefs or values?

Bring the breath of fresh air.
You can make the world a better place.

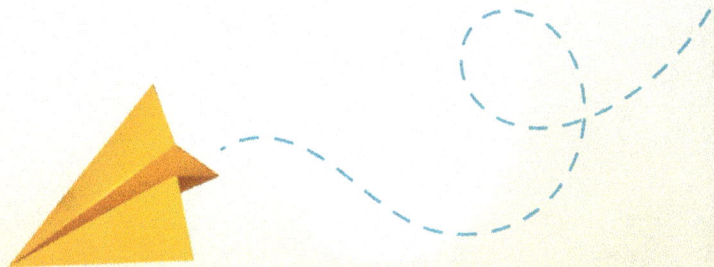

Start Noticing

*"This is the day the Lord has made.
We will rejoice and be glad in it."*

Psalm 118:24 (NLT)

I still wonder about Little Jack Horner, sitting in the corner, so focused on his pie that he misses the celebration happening around him. And then I wonder, how often do I get caught up in my own little piece of life and miss the goodness, the burning bushes, opportunities, conversations, the people woven into my ordinary days?

What if we set our tasty treat aside—our phones, our worries, our escapes—and start noticing? What would we see?

God is always showing up. But are we seeing him? Whether through sacred interruptions or quiet whispers in our soul, let's open our eyes to the wonders and miracles around us. What will you notice today?

Dear Friend, Your Thoughts?

- What did you notice this week that caused you to smile, or giggle, or simply brought you moments of joy or beauty?

- Think back over your last few days. What burning bush, conversation, or glimpse of beauty might you have missed? What distractions or habits kept you from noticing moments of goodness?

- What steps can you take to become more aware of God's presence in the people, places, and events around you?

Life is filled with wonder and miracles. Notice them.

Dental Drama

"Casting all your cares [all your anxieties, all your worries, and all your concerns, once and for all] on Him, for He cares about you [with deepest affection, and watches over you very carefully]."

I Peter 5:7 (AMP)

Dental anxiety is real. Am I right? I have a friend who claims a dental appointment feels like a spa day. She's so relaxed she actually falls asleep in the chair. Meanwhile, I'm over here white-knuckling the armrests!

But anxiety doesn't just appear when we're facing the dreaded drill or catching sight of those rebellious chin hairs that are long enough to braid. No, anxiety can run a lot deeper, quietly weaving its way into our souls during life's more serious moments too.

Here's the good news. You don't have to face life's frustrations and struggles alone. Invite God into your big, scary thing. He genuinely cares about it! He can kick your fear to the curb and fill you with his perfect peace.

And then? Look for the Amandas in your life. Those courageous encouragers who walk alongside you through the hard stuff. Sometimes she'll bring you that magical tweezer with a built-in light (bless her!), and other times she'll offer a listening ear and words that lift your spirit exactly when you need them most.

Dear Friend, Your Thoughts?

- Who has been an Amanda—a Courageous Encourager—in your life? (How about sending her a quick thank-you this week?) Who needs you to be her Amanda today?

- What truths from Scripture can you hold on to when fear feels overwhelming? Write down a few Bible verses that you can quickly go to when life feels hard.

- What practical steps can you take to invite God's peace into your "big scary" situations?

When you are afraid, whisper the name that has the power to banish that fear. Simply whisper, "Jesus."

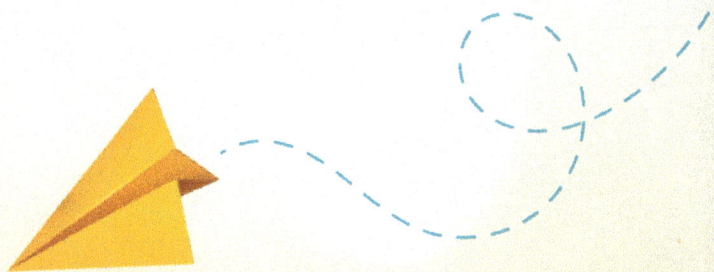

Get Out of the Rut

"Are you tired? Worn out? Burned out on religion? Come to me. Get away with me and you'll recover your life. I'll show you how to take a real rest. Walk with me and work with me—watch how I do it. Learn the unforced rhythms of grace."

Matthew 11:28-29 (MSG)

You've probably had one of those days when nothing's wrong but everything's wrong, right? Those gray, blah days when you're stuck in a rut so deep you could plant potatoes in it. Oh, friend, those days show up for all of us.

What have I learned? Most of the time, it's up to me to get myself out of those gloomies. (Bummer, I know. Wouldn't it be nice to have a magic wand that changes everything?) I need to change my stinkin' thinkin'. Get out of my comfy-but-frumpy sweatpants, straighten up, and wake up my body. Change my scenery which helps change my perspective. And never ever forget that Jesus promises me—us—a full life. There's joy and newness waiting for us on the other side of the gloom. Let's go!

P.S. Just a reminder: sometimes we need some help kicking out the sides of the rut we're in. Talk to someone that offers professional help. That's always a smart decision.

Dear Friend, Your Thoughts?

- When life looks gray and you're feeling tired and gloomy, which of these blah-influencers is most likely taking up space in your heart?

  > You're tired.

  > You're ignoring God.

  > You're bored—in a rut.

- What steps can you take to deal with that blah-influencer(s)?

- What small change could you make today to bring joy or excitement into your routine? Maybe it's a physical action you take that brightens your day. Like a favorite sweater, phone call with a friend, Spandex capris!, etc. What could be your go-to, get-out-of-the-rut day brightener?

God never intended for us to live a listless, restless life—a boring life. Kick the sides out of your rut. Experience the full life God has for you!

Back to the Basics

"I love the Lord because he hears my voice and my prayer for mercy."

Psalm 116:1 (NLT)

You know, I've been walking with God for many years. And still, even after seeing his faithfulness over and over, I sometimes catch myself wondering if he's cozied up in a storm shelter while I'm out here clinging to a tree branch, trying not to become Dorothy in *The Wizard of Oz*. When life gets stormy, it's so easy to get tangled up in the complicated stuff, isn't it? I find myself obsessively checking life's weather app for signs of blue sky, while missing those bright rays of sunshine already breaking through.

But here's what changes everything. In those moments when my brain is doing Olympic-level gymnastics with worry, I'm learning to quiet my heart and listen for his whispers: *I see you. I love you. I've got you.* Simple words. Basic truths. And somehow, they're exactly what my anxious heart needs to hear to remember I'm not weathering this storm alone.

Listen for his whispers. Watch for the rays of sunshine. Remember the basics.

Dear Friend, Your Thoughts?

- Which of the "faith basics" mentioned in this letter resonates most with you? (God is big. God loves me. God's grace is amazing.) Why does it connect with you?

- Reflect on Psalm 23:1–3. How does this passage speak to your current situation?

- Are there any hymns or verses that remind you of God's faithfulness? How can you incorporate them into your daily routine? Write them on a notecard? Text them into your phone? Make a note of what you're going to use to remember his faithfulness.

* My goodness. In the book, this is chapter 17. (A *second* chapter 17.) *Good grief.*

Even in our darkest moments, not everything is hopeless. Life can be extremely chaotic, but God is always present.

If God Sent You a Note

"Let me hear of your unfailing love each morning, for I am trusting you. Show me where to walk, for I give myself to you."

Psalm 143:8 (NLT)

You know that quiet smile that spreads across your face when you spot a personal letter in your mailbox? Now imagine seeing one with "From: God" in the return address. Just think about that for a moment. Wouldn't you find the quietest corner of your house, maybe curl up in your favorite chair, and take a deep breath before opening the envelope? This wouldn't be a formal memo or a stern list of instructions. No, this would be a heart-to-heart letter from The One who knows every detail of your story. Your hopes, your hurts, your dreams. The One whose love for you never dims, never wavers, never gives up.

Perhaps you'd like to settle in and read this letter again, inviting each promise to sink deep into your heart. Read it out loud, make the words personal. *"God gave me a new day today. He created it just for me."*

Every word will whisper, *I am so loved.*

Dear Friend, Your Thoughts?

- Which of God's promises in this "note from God" (peace, hope, presence, or love) feels most needed in your life today? Why?

- John 14:27 says: *"I am leaving you with a gift—peace of mind and heart."* This promise isn't just a comforting idea, it's meant to transform your everyday moments. How might your day unfold differently if you walked through it carrying this divine peace like a gift to unwrap rather than something you're still searching for?

- Write a letter back to God. Thank him for his love and invite him into your tears, your overwhelm, and your hurts.

God doesn't miss a thing about your life. He cares about every single bit of it.

Let's Do Something

"'What should I do, Lord?'
And the Lord told me, 'Get up and go.'"

Acts 22:10 (NLT)

Do you ever catch yourself living vicariously through other people's Instagram stories or the latest reality TV show while your own life sits on pause? I get it. But if we want everything God has for us, if we want to do everything he's put us on this earth to do, and if we want every good thing he has for us … we have to *do something.*

What if we stop being professional observers and become active participants instead? Let's say *Yes!* to God. Let's go. Let's do something.

Are you with me? Oh, I hope so!

Dear Friend, Your Thoughts?

- What small adventure have you taken lately that pulled you out of spectator mode? A moment when you traded watching life from the sidelines for jumping right into experiencing something new?

- It's so easy to slip into our cozy little routines, isn't it? Those favorite foods, familiar routes, and predictable choices that feel safe. What's that one risky thing that keeps nudging at your soul? The one that makes your stomach flutter but might just bring that spark back to your eyes if you dared to try it.

- Banning Liebscher wrote: "The only difference between those who did something for God and those who didn't was that those who did something for God did something."* What action is God calling you to take?

---

*Banning Liebscher, *The Three-Mile Walk: The Courage You Need to Live the Life God Wants for You* (Grand Rapids, Michigan: Zondervan, 2020), 69.

If we want to do something for God, we need to do something.

Feeling Invisible

"O Lord, you have examined my heart and know everything about me.
You know when I sit down or stand up ... You know everything I do ...
You place your hand of blessing on my head."

Psalm 139:1-5 (NLT)

Remember how excited those kids were as they scrambled to hear the children's sermon? All that skipping and waving and pure joy as they looked for the cameras focused on them? We miss that as we get older, don't we? It's like we've poured ourselves into serving, loving, and showing up, yet somehow, we've faded into the background.

Here's the truth. Being unseen by people doesn't mean you're unseen by God. He sees you. He always has. And when we start to believe that deep down, something shifts. The slights and the oversights don't sting as much because we know God is right there, leaning in, whispering, *I see you. You matter to me.*

Your worth isn't something that can be taken away by someone's opinion or by difficult circumstances. It's not up for debate or dependent on someone else's validation. Let that truth be a steady anchor on those days when the world tries to convince you otherwise!

Dear Friend, Your Thoughts?

- In this letter, you read Isaiah 43:1 and Ephesians 2:10. How do those truths help reshape the way you view your own significance?

- Who has been a "ray of sunshine" in your life during a tough season? How did she remind you that you are not invisible?

- What small act can you do this week to remind someone else that she is seen and valued?

No person and no situation has the power to make you insignificant. You are significant—your life matters—because God says it does.

Once Upon a Time

"The only letter of recommendation we need is you yourselves. Your lives are a letter written in our hearts; everyone can read it and recognize our good work among you. Clearly, you are a letter from Christ ..."

2 Corinthians 3:2-3 (NLT)

We've been enjoying *"Once upon a time ..."* stories for years, haven't we? Have you ever wondered what kind of story you're telling with your life? Your name may not be Sleeping Beauty, nor are you turning pumpkins into carriages, but you're writing your story every single day. And one day, someone's going to look back and finish that sentence about you: *Once upon a time, she ... What?*

Will your story tell them you fought the good fight, kept the faith, and finished the race? Or will your chapters tell them you fought others, wrote your own truths, and forgot about the race.

What kind of story are you writing?

Dear Friend, Your Thoughts?

- Whose life story has inspired you? What made their story stand out?

- What does it mean to you to "provide people with a glimpse of good living and of the living God" as described in Philippians 2:15?

- What kind of story do you hope your life tells to future generations? What values do you want to be remembered for? How do you want people to finish the story about you: *Once upon a time, she ... What?*

Fight the good fight.
Keep the faith.
Finish the race.

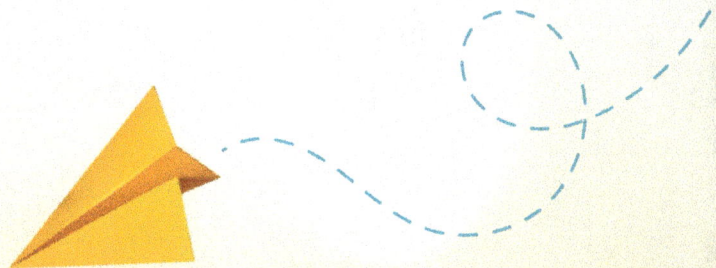

The Waiting Room

"So don't sit around on your hands! No more dragging your feet! Clear the path for long-distance runners so no one will trip and fall, so no one will step in a hole and sprain an ankle. Help each other out. And run for it!"

Hebrews 12:12-13 (MSG)

Don't you just love those self-service waiting rooms we create? You know, the ones where we've convinced ourselves we're "not quite ready" to do what God's calling us to do? We sit there mindlessly browsing through those imaginary outdated magazines, making excuses that would impress everyone else sitting in the waiting room.

But God calls us to move, even when we don't feel prepared. And we can trust his leading and his timing.

So, what's keeping you in the waiting room? Is it fear? Doubt? Or just the comfort of staying put? Maybe today isn't just another day of waiting. Maybe today is the day to get up and go.

Dear Friend, Your Thoughts?

- What waiting room are you currently sitting in? What's keeping you there? Fear, doubt, or something else?

- What small step can you take this week to leave the waiting room and move toward God's purpose for you?

- If you're striving to live so that nothing God called you to do is left undone, you're essentially saying yes to everything God asks of you. What priorities in your current season might need gentle rearranging to create more space for hearing and responding to God's callings?

We've been given this one life to live for our Jesus. It isn't a dress rehearsal for the real thing. Let's be women of faith who leave nothing undone that God has called us to do.

Behind Closed Doors

"You keep track of all my sorrows. You have collected all my tears in your bottle. You have recorded each one in your book."

Psalm 56:8 (NLT)

People are complicated, aren't they? We only see what they let us see, but behind every smile, there's a story. Some good stories, some hard, some messy. And you and I both know, we have parts of our own story we don't want the world to see, don't we?

So, what if we meet people where they really are instead of where we think they should be? What if we listened more, judged less, and just showed up with a little grace?

When we make space for real connection, we create room for healing, hope, and the kind of friendships that don't require perfect scripts or polished performances. Who in your life might need that kind of grace today?

Dear Friend, Your Thoughts?

- Who in your life might be hiding parts of their story behind "closed doors?" How can you show up for them with compassion and grace?

- Have you ever felt the need to put on a "perfect" front? How did it feel? Sometimes we put on that "perfect" front because of situations behind closed doors we're not ready to share, while other times it's simply because we don't feel "good enough" in the moment. What's one small way you've found to let your guard down and show up as your real self, even when it feels vulnerable? Or if you're still working on this (aren't we all?), what's one tiny step that feels possible for you?

- What does it mean to you that God is the "great transformer of people?" How does this truth affect how you view others' stories, and your own?

Let's meet people with grace and compassion, right where they are. God is the great transformer of people. Let him work while we love.

Salt Makes a Difference

"Be gracious in your speech. The goal is to bring out the best in others in a conversation, not put them down, not cut them out."

Colossians 4:6 (MSG)

My cooking is so awesome even the smoke alarm cheers me on! That pretty much sums up my rocky relationship with cooking. (It's also printed on a cute dishtowel a friend gave me. Love it!) But I learned a few culinary skills in my cooking masterclass, and this particular lesson amazed me: salt is a total game-changer. Who knew! And did you know that there's a whole lineup of must-have salts for every kitchen?

My meager attempts at cooking have convinced me. Salt makes a difference. And just think. If salt can transform a mediocre meal into something incredible, imagine what our words can do when they're seasoned well.

The right words can bring out the best in others. That's us being the salt. I'm all in on that! And the best part? We don't need a masterclass to season someone's day with kindness, compassion, and hope. We just start shaking it out.

Dear Friend, Your Thoughts?

- When did someone's "seasoned words" make a positive impact on your life? How did it make you feel?

- What does "seasoning well" mean in your relationships? How can you apply this principle in your everyday interactions?

- How does Colossians 4:6 inspire you to change the way you speak and connect with others?

Season your words with grace. They have the power to transform relationships.

LETTER 26
Living My Encore

"'For I know the plans I have for you,' says the Lord. 'They are plans for good and not for disaster, to give you a future and a hope.'"
Jeremiah 29:11 (NLT)

You know those musicians who come back for an encore, and *it's the best part of the whole concert*? That's what this season of life can be. Not the winding down, not the leftovers. But the big finish. The part where you show up, give it all you've got, and make these days count. Remember, God is still at work, still writing, still inviting you to step forward with faith and anticipation.

So, whether you're in your 40's, your 60's, or your 80's, bring your very best into this season of life! Lean into it like it's your exhilarating encore. Live with anticipation instead of hesitation.

What if you lived like the best is *still ahead*? I believe it is!

Dear Friend, Your Thoughts?

- Isaiah 43:18-19 reminds us to look for the new things God is doing. What new opportunities or blessings might God be putting in front of you?

- What are you excited about in this season of your life? What's filling your days with energy and meaning, like an encore that sticks with you long after the applause fades?

- Give a title to your encore presentation. What would you call this next vibrant piece of music that's waiting to be written?

I want to live
my life's encore well.
Savor every note played.
Embrace each moment.
Eagerly anticipate
what's ahead.

Let's Start a Movement

"For the Lord God is our sun and our shield. He gives us grace and glory. The Lord will withhold no good thing from those who do what is right. O Lord of Heaven's Armies, what joy for those who trust in you."

Psalm 84:11-12 (NLT)

"Yet I am confident I will see the Lord's goodness while I am here in the land of the living."

Psalm 27:13 (NLT)

Do you ever feel like your days just … happen? You wake up, go through the motions, and before you know it, another week has passed. I get it. But what if we changed that? What if we …

- Started showing up for life, rather than waiting for life to show up?

- Started seeing the sacred in our everyday moments, rather than looking for the spectacular?

- Started participating in life, rather than observing it?

- Started embracing our days through a lens of expectation, ready to notice the beauty, the blessings, and the moments God places in front of us?

So, what do you say? Let's stop just getting through the day and start living like we actually expect something good to happen. Then notice what God is doing!

Dear Friend, Your Thoughts?

- Consider the promises (that are kept!) in the verses above. What's the message for YOU in those verses?

- How often do you pause in your typical "ordinary day" to notice God's presence in it? What might happen if you begin each day with *God, what good things do you have for me today?*

- "Just getting through the day" has become a way of life for many. Why do you think that is? Are you ready to embrace a lifestyle that reflects more hope and possibility? What will that take?

If someone whispered to me right now, "There has to be more to life," I'd whisper back, "You bet there is!"

Courageous Encouragers

"My counsel for you is simple and straightforward: Just go ahead with what you've been given. You received Christ Jesus, the Master; now live him. You're deeply rooted in him. You're well constructed upon him. You know your way around the faith. Now do what you've been taught. School's out; quit studying the subject and start living it! And let your living spill over into thanksgiving."

Colossians 2:6-7 (MSG)

You know what takes real courage? Encouraging someone else when you're not even sure you've got it all together yourself. But that's exactly what we're called to do. Show up, notice, and remind someone they're not alone. It doesn't have to be big. Just a text, a smile, a *Hey, I see you, and I'm cheering for you.* Those little things matter more than we realize.

What if we became the kind of women who did that? The ones who encourage boldly, love generously, and keep showing up? We can ignite hope, bring healing, and make a difference in our homes, workplaces, and communities.

Does it sound like a movement you want to be part of? I bet it does. I'm with you.

Let's get up and go.

Let's be Courageous Encouragers.

Dear Friend, Your Thoughts?

- What specific fear has been whispering *not yet* when your heart feels called to encourage someone? What might happen if you took that brave first step anyway?

- Think of a time when you pushed past hesitation to encourage someone else. How did that small act of courage ripple outward in ways you didn't expect?

- What does becoming a Courageous Encourager look like in your everyday life this week? Name one person who needs your specific style of encouragement right now.

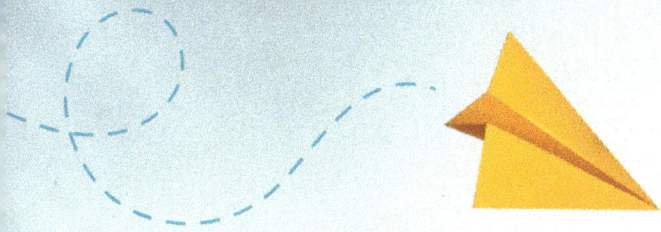

Someone in your life needs encouragement today. Bring the words that soothe, heal, and offer hope. Be the Courageous Encourager.

Themes of Encouragement

Say Yes! to God: Anticipate His Goodness

Life is good.

I believe that with every fiber in my being.

I believe good things happen to everybody. That love, grace, and mercy are ours for the asking. That no one is hopeless. That, without exception, every person matters and has the chance to live a life of significance. I believe in do-overs and begin-agains. Not just for bad hair color mishaps but for the moments that become the first words in a brand-new chapter of our stories.

Every day, hundreds of little blessings pop up on our path. And tomorrow, the sun will come up, bringing fresh promises with it. Colors, words, laughter, and moments make life exciting and extraordinary.

(And yes, I also believe that the Minnesota Vikings will one day win the Super Bowl, that sea-salt milk chocolate-covered caramels have zero calories, and arms and thighs that jiggle will one day be a fashion statement. But I might be getting carried away. So, back on message.)

The thing is, life has a way of throwing curveballs at our good moments. Cranky people get in the way. Disappointments creep in. Dreams crack. Hurtful words land where they shouldn't. Sometimes the vibrant colors of life fade to drab, and heavy clouds block the sunshine.

When those bumps start coming, I catch myself fretting and whining, murmuring, *Whoever said "life is good" needs to have their head examined.*

Good grief.

So I'm learning—still learning—how to hold on to my core belief that life is good while navigating the not-so-good and the you've-got-to-be-kidding-me moments. Some of these moments are just annoying, while others challenge the very definition of tragedy and evil.

To make sense of it all, I need to know exactly why I believe life is good. Because that's where my confidence finds its roots.

This foundational belief was born in the living room of a 2-storied, white, square house in Climax, Minnesota. It grew through simple songs like "Jesus Loves Me," memorizing Psalm 23, and reading *Little Visits with God* before bedtime.

But it didn't stop there. I *saw* it lived out—in real life, in real time—through my parents. Parents who experienced so much deep pain and heartache. The kind of hardship that would have made most people hang a For Sale sign on their faith and just walk away. Instead, in their hardest moments, they chose to believe and teach us, that *no matter what, God is faithful. We will say yes to God.*

That belief became my traveling companion. I tucked it into my suitcases, used it as a bookmark in my favorite books, and wrote my story around it. Sure, there were times I left it at a rest stop when life got ugly and "good" seemed like a foreign language. Those seasons forced me to really examine what I meant when I whispered *life is good*. It had to be more than a phrase, more than my parents' beliefs. More than what I thought I *should* say.

Over the past few decades, as I've gotten to know God better, my heart has settled on this deeply-rooted reason I can say *life is good*: **because God is good. And he only desires good things for me.**

And so, I choose—intentionally, every day—to say yes to God.

And that brings us to my book, *Anticipate God's Goodness: Letters of Encouragement to Ignite Your Spirit*, and this companion guide, *Reignite Your Spirit!*

In these pages, I'm inviting you to **say yes to God.** To recommit to following him. To see life fresh through the lens of his Word.

I'm offering you space to **reflect on God's goodness** in your own life. To recognize it, hold onto it, and let it shape your days. And on the days when there isn't a pep rally with enough pep to keep you moving, open up and re-read one of the letters in *Anticipate God's Goodness* to help you keep going.

Think of me as a friend linking arms with you as we move between joy, despair, questions, and resolve. Our moods may swing like a pendulum, and our faith might get as flaky as a bad case of dandruff. But here's the thing. **God is steadfast. He never leaves. Never quits. He always has good things for us, today and just around the corner.**

Session #1 Letters

Dear Friend, Your Thoughts?

- Like the women racing in the triathlon, have you ever done something brave, even if you weren't ready? When you knew it wouldn't be the best or perfect?

- What's your maybe-one-day dream that you can't stop thinking about? That idea you'd love to explore. The adventure you'd like to take.

  > What's keeping you from giving it a try?

  > What is one thing you could do this week to move forward on it?

- What "race" in your life feels daunting right now? What fears or excuses are holding you back from taking action? As a group, share truths—Bible verses— that can replace those fears.

- When you feel unsettled or anxious, what practical steps can you take to invite God into those moments?

- Why is it hard for us to get rid of the weeds in our hearts? To ask God to point out anything that offends him. What are we afraid of? Is that fear based on a lie, or is it based on God's promises and truth? Does that fear align with what we believe about God?

- What words or phrases in "If God Sent You a Note" (Letter 19) spoke directly to your heart? Why?

- What single message from God is ringing clearest in your heart right now? If you carried just one truth forward from everything you've read here—that whisper that feels like it was meant especially for you—what would it be?

Get Up & Go: Live as a Courageous Encourager

Sometimes, that little nudge to get up and go—to actually *do* something—shows up when we least expect it. You know what I mean?

This was one of those moments.

It was college week at Myrtle Beach. The sand was packed with young adults, all trying *very hard* to look like they weren't trying at all. You could spot it from a mile away. The casual-but-not-really glances and that "I wish I looked cooler" energy radiating from little clusters of people checking to see who's noticing them. We could practically see the thought bubbles above their heads: *Is anyone watching? Do I look okay? Am I doing this right?*

(Quick side note: My sisters and I could not, for the life of us, keep our mouths from hanging open as we took in the *bold* approach to beachwear. My heavens. It was as if fabric had gone extinct. I mean, were these girls actually comfortable, or were they extremely dedicated to their tan lines? Or maybe this was just a dedicated act of bravery? I can't
even ...)

But anyway, back to my story.

Late one afternoon, once the spring break crowd had headed back to their party spots, I noticed a surfer carrying a bright blue board, edging his way into the Atlantic. Except, he never actually surfed.

He'd wade out, bob around a bit, drift with the current, then walk back to shore. Rinse and repeat. No riding waves, no attempts, just ... waiting. He had a chance to say he'd surfed in the Atlantic Ocean, to have that moment of *doing* something. Holding all the potential for adventure in his hands, and did nothing with it.

That hit me. Because I saw my reflection in his blue surfboard.

How many times have I done exactly that? God hands me an assignment, an opportunity. I've got everything I need right in front of me. His promises, every reason to go for it. And what do I do? I wade. I float. Watch. Wonder. I ask myself, *Is anyone watching? Do I look okay? Am I doing this right? Am I brave enough?*

You too?

Sigh.

We miss out on so much when we ignore God's promptings.

Deep down, you and I both know that our excuses are pretty weak, aren't they? I mean, really. When God gives us both the nudge and the tools, when he's equipped us with exactly what we need, no excuse really holds water. No excuse is good enough.

Fear? Not feeling ready or good enough? Worried about what people might say? Concerned that we might do it wrong? Waiting for our ducks to get in a row?

Here's the truth I keep going back to. When we make these excuses, we're basically saying that we trust our own shaky understanding, our own experiences and emotions, our own strength, more than God's rock-solid promises to be with us, support us, and guide us. *Oh, Lord, have mercy.*

But when we are brave enough to look beyond our excuses, we will realize and remember: **God has good things planned for us.** That's not just a nice thought. It's a promise he keeps. So why are we standing in knee-deep water, swishing our hands around, watching the waves roll by?

God didn't place us here, at this time, in this place, to stand still. He has something for us to do. We are part of his beautiful plan. And **we can't live out our purpose and respond to his if we refuse to move.**

You know what Bible verse has taken up permanent residence in my brain? Genesis 22:2-3, where God tells Abraham:

"'Take your son, your only son—yes, Isaac, whom you love so much—and go to the land of Moriah. Go and sacrifice him as a burnt offering on one of the mountains, which I will show you.' The next morning Abraham got up early. He saddled his donkey."

Oh my. Can you imagine? No second-guessing, no negotiating with God, no *but I'm not ready!* Just trust and action. **Abraham got up and saddled his donkey.**

That's what I want. To be like Abraham. Because trying to explain to God that now isn't the right time? That's about as effective as trying to surf without getting wet. It's just plain silly. When God says *get up and go*, I want to trust his promises and move.

I want to get up and saddle my donkey.

How about you?

You've said Yes! to God. You're committed to following Him. **Now it's time for the next step—moving.**

Here's a gentle kick-in-the-pants verse that might be just the nudge you and I need:

"My counsel for you is simple and straightforward:
Just go ahead with what you've been given.
You received Christ Jesus, the Master; now live him.
You're deeply rooted in him.
You're well constructed upon him. You know your way around the faith.
Now do what you've been taught.
School's out; quit studying the subject and start living it!
And let your living spill over into thanksgiving."

Colossians 2:6-7 (MSG)

And because God's Word is just that good, here's one more nudge:

"Here's another way to put it:
You're here to be light, bringing out the God-colors in the world.
God is not a secret to be kept. We're going public with this, as public as a city on a hill.
If I make you light-bearers, you don't think I'm going
to hide you under a bucket, do you?
I'm putting you on a light stand.
Now that I've put you there on a hilltop, on a light stand—shine!
Keep open house; be generous with your lives.
By opening up to others,
you'll prompt people to open up with God, this generous Father in heaven."

Matthew 5:14-16 (MSG)

The images and words are crystal clear in my mind: the memory of the young man standing in the shallow ocean water, holding his board. Abraham's trust and obedience. God's clear direction and the promises in his Word. I need no other convincing.

I'm kicking my excuses to the curb.

It's time to move.

Session #2 Letters

Dear Friend, Your Thoughts?

- How was Abraham able to "get up and saddle his donkey" after God told him what to do? What do you suppose had prepared him for his obedience?

- We've all had those moments when we wonder if we belong in a particular room or situation. Perhaps you can relate to the Israelites when they felt like grasshoppers being led by a grasshopper god. When have you felt that way? What's behind that feeling?

- Madeleine L'Engle writes about showing others a "lovely light" in Letter 14. What does that look like in your daily interactions?

- What small step can you take this week to leave the "waiting room" and move toward God's purpose for you?

- Think about the unique ways you bring joy to others. How can you continue to share those gifts this week?

- Banning Liebscher wrote: "The only difference between those who did something for God and those who didn't was that those who did something for God did something."* What action is God calling you to take?

- What single message from God is ringing clearest in your heart right now? If you carried just one truth forward from everything you've read here—that whisper that feels like it was meant especially for you—what would it be?

* Banning Liebscher, *The Three-Mile Walk: The Courage You Need to Live the Life God Wants for You* (Grand Rapids, Michigan: Zondervan, 2020), 69.

Get Up & Go: Live as a Courageous Encourager

Session #3 Letters

Dear Friend, Your Thoughts?

- Who showed up to sync swim with you when you needed a little push or a gentle lift? What kind of encouragement and support did she offer?

- How can you shift from observing the lives of others (on social media, TV, books, etc.) to actively participating in your own life? What small step(s) could you take today?

- What can you do to become more aware of God's presence in the people, places, and events around you?

- What does "seasoning well" mean in your relationships? How can you apply this principle in your everyday interactions?

- What are the needs you notice in front of you? What skills, experiences, or gifts have you been given that could meet those needs? Will you get up and go?

- What single message from God is ringing clearest in your heart right now? If you carried just one truth forward from everything you've read here—that whisper that feels like it was meant especially for you—what would it be?

Keep Going: Rest With Your Sneakers On

There are moments that cannot be erased from my memory bank.

My eyes can't unsee what I saw, and my muscles can't forget what they endured.

Let's take a little stroll back to the 1970s. High school gymnasium. Physical Education class.

We had to wear those one-piece, royal blue gym uniforms with elastic around the waist, elastic around the arms, elastic around the thighs, and snaps up the front. I *mean, really!* Did the designer have any clue that there was absolutely nothing attractive, flattering, or remotely breathable about this piece of clothing?

As if that fashion crime wasn't humiliating enough, we had to exercise to the legendary, painfully peppy "Chicken Fat" song. Yes, that was a thing. The goal? To "give that chicken fat back to the chicken" while we flailed through floor exercises. "Go, you chicken fat, go away! Go, you chicken fat, go!" *

Who, in the name of all things healthy and fashionable, thought this was a good idea? Michelin Man-inspired uniforms and a motivational poultry anthem.

That brings us to the grand finale. The annual Presidential Fitness Test.

Every spring, we had to endure a fitness assessment that included sit-ups, pull-ups, flexibility stretches, and, worst of all, running. In my small hometown, we ran laps around the bus track behind the school. I can't tell you exactly how many times we circled that gravel road, but I can tell you it felt like we were training to run to Nebraska.

After the first several hundred feet, my knees and thighs started protesting. A little farther, and my lungs joined the revolution. The more everything hurt, the more I obsessed over the pain. (*Oh, my poor knee ... My lungs might actually explode ... This is ridiculous ... I think my leg is falling off!*)

That's when I'd hit my breaking point. I'd had enough. I started wondering, *would anyone notice if I just laid down on this horrible gravel road and took a nap?* Yup. I was ready to quit. Who would care? I was tired, saw absolutely no purpose in this torture, and quitting felt like the most reasonable option in the history of reasonable options.

Fast forward to today. Some days, doesn't it feel like we're still running around that track? Trying to catch our breath. Wondering how we're supposed to finish this race

called life.

Then we read again those words in Ephesians 4:1 that call us to be Courageous Encouragers:

"Here's what I want you to do. While I'm locked up here, a prisoner for the Master, I want you to get out there and walk—better yet, run!—on the road God called you to travel. I don't want any of you sitting around on your hands. I don't want anyone strolling off, down some path that goes nowhere." (MSG)

Walk? Run? Travel? What about my nap?

You've been there, right? Maybe you're there now.

You're tired. Maybe more than tired—you're weary. Worn out.

May I encourage you from the very bottom of my heart?

Good. OK. Lean in and listen.

Don't quit. Don't give up.

Instead, determine what's causing your weariness, and figure out what you need to regain your equilibrium and energy.

The farm girl in me knows that for something to grow, the roots have to go deep. So instead of frantically trying to fix what's going on around you, **pay attention to what's happening inside your precious heart.**

And while you're at it, ditch the royal blue jumpsuit and anything else that makes it hard to breathe. Let go of those lies that have made themselves at home in your mind, the ones that keep you spinning and swirling and make everything feel foggy. Find your favorite cozy chair, take a deep breath, and take stock of your schedule, your commitments, those sneaky time-wasters (trust me, I get this!), and **what's actually *filling* your tank.**

Stop trying to fix what isn't yours to fix. Go back to the basics. Ask God what's true. **Get out of the rut you've worn into the ground.**

I know what you're probably thinking: That's easy to say. A whole lot harder to do.

You're right.

So let me take your sweet face in my hands, look you in the eye, and remind you of something important. **You are not God. You don't have to live, work, or serve in your own strength. Let go of the weight you were never meant to carry. Invite Jesus into this moment and let him do the heavy lifting.**

Take a nap. But keep your sneakers on.

You need rest. You need refreshment. You need renewal. And then, you'll be ready to keep going.

Starting a race is easy. Finishing is the hard part. But here's the thing. This race, this life we're living, isn't a marathon, or a sprint, or even a brisk walk. It's movement. It's moving in faith. And right now? **You're just stopping at the refreshment stand, doing what you need to do so you can get up and go again.**

When my energy tank hits empty, when my enthusiasm has disappeared and I still have gravel road laps to go, here's what helps: I talk to a friend. And I say something like this:

I'm tired. Nothing's wrong but everything's wrong. I just want the swirling to stop for a minute so I can catch my breath. I want things to be fixed. I don't need you to fix them. I don't even know what I'm asking or why I'm telling you this. But I just need someone to know that I'm worn out.

Then I slow down. Breathe. **I let my friend be my courageous encourager.** And I ask my heart what it needs to feel nourished. (It knows.)

God is a good God.

Life can be hard.

And a hard life doesn't change the fact that God is a good God.

Oh, dear friend. **You are loved by a God whose love never quits.** He never gives up on you. He never stops calling you to walk with him.

YOU are someone who is loved. Even when you don't feel it.

YOU are someone who is gifted and talented. Even when you don't see it.

YOU are someone who brings something special into this world. Even when you don't know it.

So take that nap.

Keep your sneakers on.

* "Chicken Fat," written by Meredith Willson and performed by Robert Preston, 1962. Commissioned by the President's Council on Physical Fitness under President John F. Kennedy.

Session #4 Letters

Dear Friend, Your Thoughts?

- Think about the "extra weight" slowing you down. What distractions or unnecessary commitments might you need to let go of?

- What activities, people, or practices bring you the most energy and joy? How can you create more time for them in your daily life?

- Psalm 23 is so refreshing, isn't it? What do "quiet pools" and "lush meadows" look like for you? Where do you find them?

- Discouragement can feel subtle and sneaky. How can you remain alert to recognize it? How will you shove it back into its box when you recognize it?

- John 14:27 speaks about the gift of peace Jesus gives us. What steps can you take to claim that peace in your daily life?

- Which of the "faith basics" in Letter 18 resonates most with you? (God is big. God loves me. God's grace is amazing.) Why does it connect with you?

- What single message from God is ringing clearest in your heart right now? If you carried just one truth forward from everything you've read here—that whisper that feels like it was meant especially for you—what would it be?

* My goodness. I have two chapter 17's in the book, and no chapter 18. "Back to the Basics" is the second chapter 17.

Keep Going: Rest With Your Sneakers On

Session #5 Letters

Dear Friend, Your Thoughts?

- Dallas Willard encourages us to arrange our days to "experience total contentment, joy, and confidence … with God."* How can you incorporate this perspective into your daily life?

- Psalm 116:9 reminds us to walk in the Lord's presence. What practices help you stay connected to Him throughout your day?

- What change could you make today to bring joy or excitement into your routine? What could be your go-to, get-out-of-the-rut day brightener?

- Isaiah 43:18-19 reminds us to look for the new things God is doing. What new opportunities or blessings might God be putting in front of you?

- Give a title to your encore presentation. What would you call this next vibrant piece of music that's waiting to be written?

- How are you going to show up as a Courageous Encourager? Really think about how you can use your gifts and serve the people God places in front of you. YOU will make a difference!

- What single message from God is ringing clearest in your heart right now? If you carried just one truth forward from everything you've read here—that whisper that feels like it was meant especially for you—what would it be?

* John Ortberg, *Soul Keeping: Caring for the Most Important Part of You* (Grand Rapids, Michigan: Zondervan, 2014), 98.

Dear Friend

Consider this a P.S. to all my letters. A final note from the bottom of my heart!

Well, here we are at the end of our journey through *Reignite Your Spirit!* But you know, I don't think of this as an ending at all. More like a launching pad. A starting line. A "step out of the pew and experience God's goodness" moment!

Remember when you first started working through this guide? Maybe you were feeling a little weary. A bit stuck. Perhaps wondering if your everyday, ordinary life could really shine with spirit and anticipation.

But here we are! You've plowed fields, filled empty tanks, pushed past those waiting room excuses, and remembered that you belong exactly where God has placed you. You've popped bubbles of shame, gotten settled in his presence, and learned to stop struggling against the waves. You've been reminded that even when life's ducks refuse to cooperate (mine are splashing around in complete chaos today, by the way), God is faithful.

I'm so excited for you!

Why? Because taking this journey wasn't just about reading some letters or answering a few questions. It was about saying Yes! to God in big and small ways. It was about **recognizing that your life—yes, YOURS—is a race worth running, a story worth telling, an encore worth living.**

So now what? Where do we go from here?

Well, **first, consider what you've learned.** Sit back and leaf through those notes of yours. What nuggets have you uncovered about yourself? What dreams are feeling closer to becoming a reality? Something really possible. What gifts have been sitting in the corner of your heart, wrapped and ready, just waiting for permission to be opened?

And now, it's time. Time to trade those comfy slippers for sneakers. **Time to get up and go.**

Maybe for you, that means finally stepping into that dream God's been nudging you toward. Perhaps it's reaching out to someone who needs a Courageous Encourager in her corner. Or maybe—and this is important—it's giving yourself permission to rest with your sneakers on before you jump back into the race.

Whatever your next step looks like, remember that you're not taking it alone. The God who hangs the stars and names them is walking beside you, his hand gently on your shoulder. He's already prepared good works for you to do, and he's provided everything you need to do them.

I'm cheering for you too! I'm over here waving my pompoms, believing that your Yes! to God is going to create ripples you can't even imagine. Isn't that cool?

So let's make a pact, you and me. Let's agree to:

- Start showing up for life instead of waiting for life to show up
- Trade our hesitation for anticipation
- Look for burning bushes in our ordinary days
- Be the salt that brings out the best in others
- Keep skipping with joy, even when others try to shush us
- Remember that even fairy tales get messy
- Get out of the rut when we find ourselves stuck
- Live our encore with enthusiasm and purpose
- Be a Courageous Encourager who notices needs and meets them

Life is happening right now. In your messy kitchen, your work cubicle, your cozy chair, your Tuesday afternoon meetings, your Saturday morning errands. **God is there in all of it, inviting you to see his faithfulness, to anticipate his goodness, and to participate rather than just observe.**

So grab that surfboard of yours and actually ride the waves. Put on your royal blue gym suit (well, maybe not!) and run the race marked out for you. Saddle your donkey like Abraham and move when God says move.

Your story isn't finished yet.

In fact, I have a feeling the best chapters are still ahead.

With so much love and a heart full of anticipation for all God has in store for you,

Gaye

P.S. I'd love to hear how God is working in your life. Drop me a note and let me know how you're saying Yes! to him, how you're getting up and going, and how you keep going as a Courageous Encourager. Your story matters to me!

Say Yes! to God: Anticipate His Goodness

Get Up & Go: Live as a Courageous Encourager

Keep Going: Rest with Your Sneakers On

Let's Stay Connected

www.GayeLindfors.com

Gaye@Gayelindfors.com

Facebook (@GayeLindforsAuthor)

Instagram (@GayeLindfors)

YouTube videos (@GayeLindfors)